Things To Do On A Rainy Day

THINGS TO DO
ON A RAINY DAY

Creative Activities for Children

By Dean Walley

Illustrated by John Overmyer

Designed by Frances Yamashita

Photographed by Nate Accardo

👑 Hallmark Children's Editions

Things To Do On A Rainy Day

MAKE A POTATO FACE

Your mother does a lot of things with potatoes. She makes mashed potatoes and french fries and potato pancakes. You can do something funny with a potato. Make a potato face. It's easy. All you need are some toothpicks,

some cloves, three carrot slices,

a little wad of cotton

and, of course,
a potato.

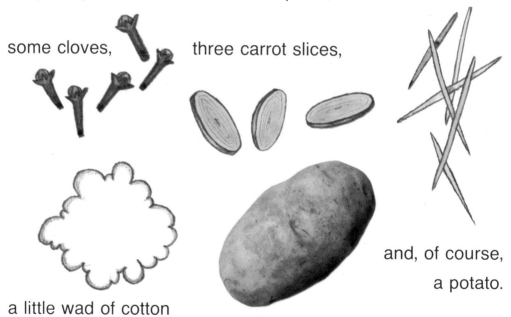

Stick toothpicks into the potato where
you think the eyes and nose
should be. Leave a little bit
of the toothpick sticking out.

Stick on two carrot eyes and a carrot nose.

Cloves make a good potato mouth.

Stick them in to make a happy mouth.

Or a grouchy mouth if you want to.

Put the cotton on top.
Stick it on with a toothpick.
Now Mr. Potato Face has hair.

He's glad he didn't turn out to be a mashed potato!

If you have to stay inside and you don't have anyone to play with, it's fun to have a pretend friend. It can be a boy or a girl. The name is up to you. You could call him Jimmy or Charley or anything you like. If it's a girl, give her a girl's name.

Show your pretend friend around your house. He'll want to see your room and all your toys. And he'll want to see your secret hideout, if you have one. Pretend friends are especially good at keeping your secrets.

A pretend friend is fun to play games with. He likes to play the same games you like to play, but he's not as good as you are. Let him win sometimes to make him feel good.

Ask mother to set an extra place at the table for your pretend friend. No need to serve him real food. Pretend friends always eat pretend food.

This is a fun way to make funny faces out of old magazine pictures. Find some old magazines — the kind that have slick paper. Look for pictures of people. With an ordinary eraser you can erase their eyes, their noses, their mouths — anything you like. Then you can draw the people any way you want to.

You can give them tiny eyes and big toothy mouths to make them look silly. Or you can give them sharp teeth and creepy eyes like monsters have!

If you'll promise to put everything away when you're through,
your mother may let you play with her button box. It will be full
of buttons of all different shapes and colors. Why not arrange
them in rows by size and color. You can thumbtack them on a
piece of cardboard to make the outline of a face or a house or
a tree or many other objects.

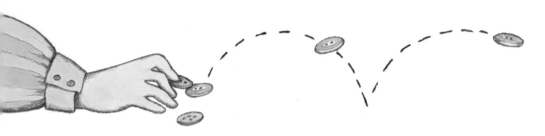

   You can make buttons hop around like tiddily winks. Put
them on the floor or on the kitchen table and snap one button
against the edge of another button. See how far you can make
a button hop. Can you hop it into a cup?

Get a long piece of thread and you can make a button necklace or a button belt. Just slip the thread through the little holes in the buttons. When the thread is full of buttons, tie the ends together in a knot. Put the buttons around your neck and you'll have a pretty necklace!

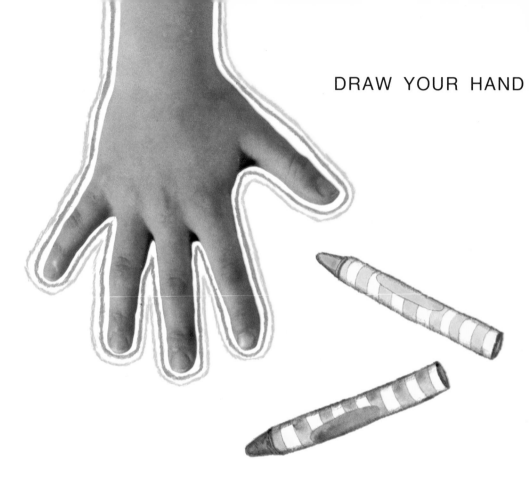

Put your hand on a piece of white paper and trace around it.
Now you have the outline of a hand just like yours. Draw some
fingernails like yours onto the outline.

Color your hand whatever way you want to. Would you like to have one blue finger and one red finger and one white finger and one yellow finger and a polka-dot thumb? Then go ahead and color it that way!

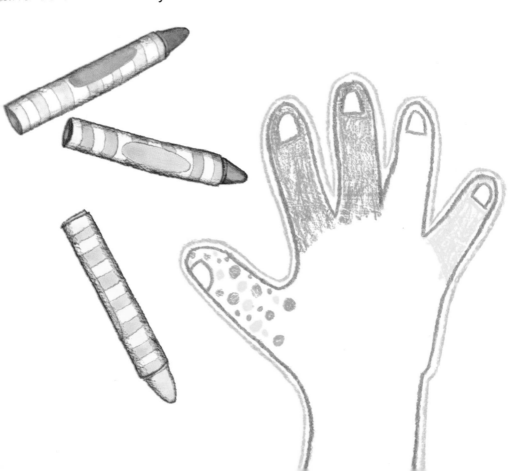

You can spend the whole afternoon playing with an old blanket. Put it over a little table and you have a tent. You can put some of your secret things in there and play inside.

Put the blanket over your head and you're a ghost. Be careful when you walk around. It's hard for a ghost to see.

Wrap it around you and you look like a mummy. Lay the blanket on the floor and pretend it's your own private island. An island is a good place to bring your toys and your pet. After you've had fun with your blanket, you can wrap it around you and take a nap.

You can make music without any fancy musical instruments. All you need are some glasses,

some water

and a spoon.

Fill the glasses with water — a lot in the first glass, not quite so much in the next, a little less in the next, and so on, until in the last glass there is just a little bit of water. Now hit each glass gently with the spoon. Each one makes a different sound. With a little practice you can play a song. Try Jingle Bells.

Maybe you can make up some songs of your own!

Every once in a while, it's fun to have a noisy. Ask mother first. She won't mind if you tell her it will just last a minute. When you have a noisy, you can yell as loud as you like. It's good to have some old pans to beat on. Drums are good, too. Be sure that you stamp your feet.

Be as noisy as you can—but just for a little while. Then have a quiet. It's good to be quiet after you have a noisy.

You have to take a bath anyway. Why not make it fun! Ask your mother for an old paint brush. Then you can paint the tub's sides with soap. Or paint yourself. That's a good way to get clean.

You can make little fountains in the bathtub. Make a little box with your hands. Leave a small opening for the water to get in and out. Now hold your hands under the water. When they are full of water, squeeze! You've made a fountain. How high can your fountain go?

The bathtub is a good place to blow bubbles. You can do it with a bubble pipe, but if you don't have one you can do it with your hands. Just put your thumb and forefinger together and dip your hand in the soapy water. Then blow!

It's fun to have ducks and ships in the tub with you. Then you can have races. Don't forget to wash behind your ears!

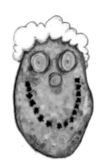